THE GRAND MINIMA

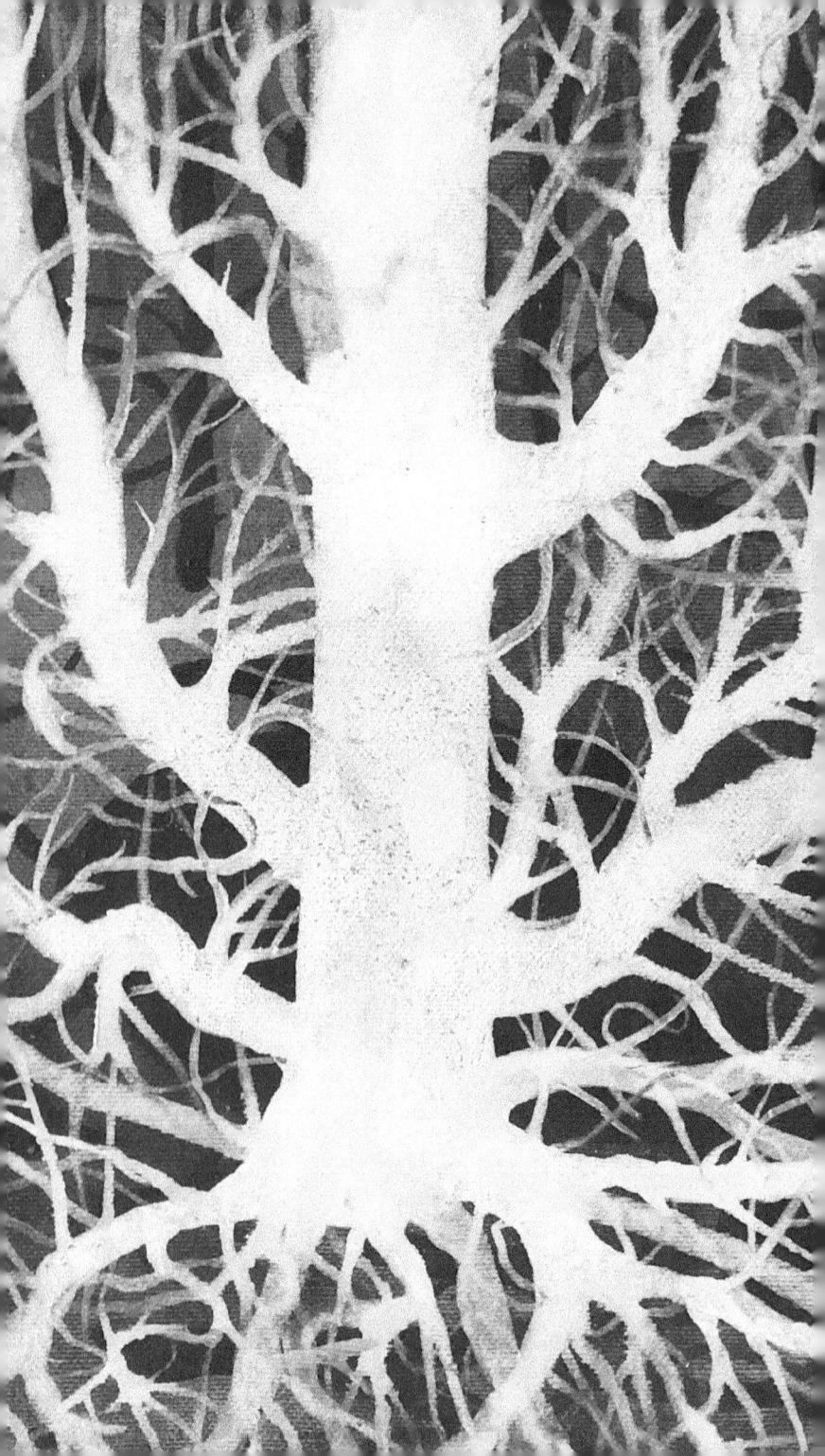

THE GRAND MINIMA

New poems 2024-2025

Todd Swift

MAIDA VALE PUBLISHING

Dedicated to my mother,
Mary Margaret (Hume) Swift

First published in 2025
by Maida Vale Publishing Ltd
Black Spring Press Group
United Kingdom

Typeset with artwork and graphic design by Edwin Smet
All rights reserved © 2025 Todd Swift

The right of Todd Swift to be identified as author of this work has been asserted in accordance with section 77 of the Copyright, Designs and Patents Act 1988

ISBN 978-1-917788-40-3

BLACKSPRINGPRESSGROUP.COM

Contents

Brief introduction — 8
The gift so subtle no one knew — 11
How many centuries — 12
There are days the Lord is dead, — 13
Because no one fears to damn — 14
christ i am a sweet poet, — 15
happy poetry day! — 16
The cold comes in — 17
If you ever feel small — 18
why so many selfies? — 19
Fox in the Garden: — 20
when i was finished speaking — 21
depression has more names — 22
Stage 4 — 23
i can't say otherwise — 24
Not for lack of trying — 25
Eutectic — 26
Poem for my mother who read me Frost first — 27
Rule Britannia at the Proms... — 28
we are wasted — 29
That poem by Yeats — 30
No great poem — 31
Good Friday Sonnet — 32
poetry is either a gift or a trick — 33
sniper, you have no kindness — 34
I listen to Ezra Koenig and read — 35

Music Review of Superstar's LP — 36
Wanting shade even with sun, — 37
one can think of better things — 38
Boys In The Rain, 1982 — 39
Book of Idioms — 40
a syringe drifts by — 41
Gondoliers — 42
The Grand Minima — 43
Lines from Verlaine — 45
I was a cut-rate Cohen — 46
My father when a young pop star — 47
What hasn't happened yet — 48
among the paintings — 49
We stopped writing about Easter — 50
The currency I traded in — 51
Goya — 53
The only love that never lies — 55
haven't been here in a while — 56
I shoot the rose — 57
The Mole Man — 58
Arizona — 59
Sonnet for obscure makers — 60
I have not done justice to my mother — 61

Bio, Acknowledgements — 64
Selected list of books — 64
Past praise — 66

TODD SWIFT

Brief introduction

Lyric poems have been "avant-garde" for some time – the work of Denise Riley (who I studied with) is a prime example. The high modernist, and 40s poems, whose work I have studied, and sometimes emulated, were capable of combining the personal, the emotive, the oratorical, the rhetorical, and the deeply mythic, with – sometimes – panache, irony, even camp verve, as John Ashbery wrote me in a letter to affirm. These poems, as all of my poems, live by their wits – their very momentum, which is their raison d'etre, is a formulation of how a mind in motion can continue to spin elaborations, even as it seeks to sum up. As a public speaker and debater, my best work was done when I had thirty seconds to say what needed saying, with a flourish.

It is sometimes considered naïve, too personal, and even somewhat simple-minded, to write lyrics, which may explore themes of love, death, time passing, seasons, and other "romantic" or "traditional" tropes of the poetic canon. And some poets I know, sometimes generate poems with AI, or Oulipo-style constraints, or even genetically, or atomically. A poem is nothing if not information, and therefore can pack a lot in to its seemingly small size, relatively speaking.

In my view, no poet should be dealt in, or out, of a hand, because of the cards they choose to play - there are many games, decks, suits, and strategies, and, each, in their own way, has merit. No period, period style, or style is ever beyond reuse or reimagining or reinvention. And poet-critics who abhor or disregard the value of the emotive, the confessional, or the lyrical, on the basis they may be too human, old-hat or saccharine, do not understand the long tradition of the lyric as mask, as a poetic artifice, and even sometimes an authentic utterance.

The aleatory, Dadaistic, and experimental are vital streams
of artistic re-mapping, and in my own work and anthologizing I
have always welcomed them; but they are not the only ways. The 21st
century should remain an open highway, so all voices, concerns, and
persons, can be heard. In this pamphlet, I modestly seek to extend
my own engagement with the lyric personae I generate and employ,
arising from within whatever it is I think I am, from time to time.

Maida Vale, London, May 12, 2025

The gift so subtle no one knew

The gift so subtle no one knew
he could remember every flower
he ever saw; what to do with that?
At first, he kept records — diaries,
ledgers, groaning accounts volumed
in Safestore holds — but soon thought better of that folderol;
then simply tattoos of the best of
them, but why bother when pistil,
stamen, stem already stuck inside his eyelids like, well, crazy glue;
knowledge, he learned, was all too
much of a good thing, a head like a florist's funeral, or a hothouse zoo;
he loved especially the ones that ate meat by way of flies, then thorns,
lastly those redder than red redness like a sun
overheating in a solar storm; he never expected pleasure
or payment for what he recalled,
a jungle of gardens in a mind fecund like an unnatural orchid,
more ghost than thought — but even rarest plants finally when gleaned got
pressed into his brain to grow wild there, and infinitely, decline
only in the way all dead worlds rot,
encircling dreams with caught vines.

How many centuries

did it take the tree
they ruined openly
to achieve its state

before, not even daring
to cut it down for good
wood, use of a kind,

they set it a going chaos,
having fed it gasoline
then shot it full of fire?

THE GRAND MINIMA

There are days the Lord is dead,

no sun. You want to boil eyes,
slit things; go to hell lovingly
as shadows slather themselves
on the leather-clad skin of
your biker gang sins; and you're
just a girl/boy: eighteen in head
though maybe ancient as blood
sucking can make it in years;
no tears when your crusaders
make swimming pools by sword
in a jaded land; it was planned
this way by an urbane believer;
just seasonal ennui, not evil
pistils, stamen, but oh my dears
how at compline we truly amen!

Because no one fears to damn

their eternal souls much anymore, the Purcell Canzona
falls a bit on deafer ears
than in years before, when
Waugh or Greene worried
at their beads, afraid, or worse,
betrayed, by some gnawing sense, that prayer, incense, God
would not exist without fiction —
but at least they tried, like Wouk in his way to keep a faith aflame
though this century is vile, bodies piled as images to fame,
war, self-acclaim, the fake smile
when once Gioconda meant
something else, when meaning held its meaning deep as space.

christ i am a sweet poet,

combining the coquetry
of the french maid i hide

inside my male-man side —
with a baron's shuttle diplomatic

nous — iron in a pretty pink glove
you could say — the bismarck of

punk dizzy play; i suspend
judgment, forgive debt, open

the gates to marauding fans;
teen icon, wunderkind, laureate

of dupe tom ford scents!

happy poetry day!

the bombs keep falling
the leaves keep falling
is poetry failing?
or is it an epiphenomenon?

you say it is more an epi pen,
to use for rescue when
times get rough. jab it in,
let poems do their stuff...

the bombs keep falling
the leaves keep falling;
verse is an unusual calling —
it translates the world to words

as if fresh states could coexist
with real shifting plates — enough,
it claims, to recreate;
to let the original die or decay.

The cold comes in

The cold comes in
The light goes out
The cold comes in
The light goes out
The green turns off
The dark stays on
The green turns off
The dark stays on
The park says ice
The sky just knows
The park says ice
The sky just knows
Autumn holds fast
Then snow at last

If you ever feel small

don't start — consider writer
Donna Tartt at five foot even;
or poet Thomas Hardy barely

five foot one; his 'Titanic'
will last, gargantuan –
as for tiny stature, Mr Keats

completes a list minuscule at five foot and zero —
yet is every poet's hero,
in and out of school; but wait — Charlotte

Brontë, master of the novel
standing in bare toes at four
foot nine! Her immortal genius is doing fine.

The noble minded can be pint-
sized in a suit, like Pope; so
tiny creator, retain big hope.

why so many selfies?

to see myself
as others don't — perfected
life, not art, the shelf
to find these on — me's,
everyone — gone through
filters like therapy — to be

improved, or to survive;
i never had a sense of my
shape, self, borders porous,
skin as skein, unravelling —
lines drawn around me odd —
is that a carrot or Todd,
my crayons asked in school;

some form of disorder maybe,
caused by genetic or human
touch — ill-defined, bad eyes,
i still rely on mirrors to tell
i think, have a soul; passports
to confirm my face is real; so
these photos are my birthdays.

Fox in the Garden:

A corrugated red roof
ten red episodes
a burnt red mirage
a red whisper of redness
red red red brown night
speed as an emotion
the red capture of motion
surprise in the shape
of fox-red shadows; air
turning half-red; twilit fox;
a red box ripped open
sight as a red harvest,
a scribbling brown-red
alert; the sick signal of slow
red stopping in the flower
bed; the dead redness
if an ill fox wanders in;
gardens of foxness; reading.

when i was finished speaking

i didn't thank anybody
stepped down from the podium,
undoing my lovely tie
my mother gave me, taking

off my father's jacket he bought
in Hong Kong, littering the floor
loudly with cufflinks from Uncle
Jack — inset with black jade –

and went to the back of
the vast tall auditorium still
echoing with my swift words —
tore off my purple vest, Oxford

shoes, ear by ear undid glasses
crafted in Italy — then walked
into the blizzard to dream for ever,
or never, whichever is.

depression has more names

than leaves of sand
on a beach tree — none
so true as end of August,
the summer seeping out
of a punctured year; tired
of London and yes the world
i know poetry won't save me —
it never did, it never will —
what can is August remaining,
but it goes, just to willy-nilly
return, circular logic takes
our happiest days just to dump
them back down again too late,
later, when we're older, tired,
no longer unafraid of time,
that broken bicycle pump,
always letting out the air.

Stage 4

my mother swims
the lake in her telltale red cap,
broad breaststrokes,
and I watch her as I did
when a boy; it's stoic,
but also she loves water,
and what she did when thirty
she is doing now, until.
Life is doing today what will
not happen tomorrow.
It is beautiful seeing her head
moving among the small waves;
enjoying how to survive:
keep moving, don't slip beneath;
kick your legs like a frog; breathe.

i can't say otherwise

it's truly pain
lengthwise
spear of rain,
we have lain here, lain
among dung, idling flies —
after our gods were slain

Not for lack of trying

Not for lack of trying,
or want of rain,
do I know you are dying
but cannot detain

what's down the line —
both voice and time —
rhyme stops no pain,
never lit the sin or

stopped a single chariot
from ruining love's night —
so like a child hate
all that's naturally wrong,

disease that runs riot
in your stomach like a rat;
what sickens is all —
your body made me fall

into the world rotting
inwardly opposite to me;
now I am reborn ill by disgust
for you my dear deserve

what life won't give —
which is to more live than
feel the fear of reserve go;
this brims what means to dust;

give her back as she gave, must
love rip shreds from skin distressed;
the rim of your skirt mother –
once in wedding dress.

Eutectic

They say the subject should be others, as if the distance from
one's self made it more true,
or finer, a puritanical
revulsion with the personal
and false sense of accuracy —
far observation never keener —
but for some, the political
vision is the cleaner — weird
since the world is a mud-field
mined to the hilt, but the soul
at least can be defused
with care, policed better maybe
though neither me nor we
is by ethics or method better —
what we write of is also fused
like eutectic alloys — based in difficult love; melted by neglect.

Poem for my mother who read me Frost first

The whole thing is the fact we're not okay,
The thing and the rest of it are the same corollary
It has the name of all and several sectors, sprayed,
Like lavender oil or some arcane graffiti, in display —
We're meshed up with the disappearing decay, gone
Like Spengler into the madhouse there, a fairground
Array that would make Ian Curtis moan this is the way
Not to go — we're AWOL on a precipice for Cruise
To cycle off, in cyclone, in perpetuity, as if to say,
The ground is up above, the twister is also there,
And I don't care who knows the plans of the Chief
Who holds the cards intact, the hand betrays
The eye that bulges from battle affray, from fearsome
Blown debris, it's not a good time to be staying out late,
Or even indoors, mate, stay somewhere else, sick bay?
The tree that hid us from the storm has been struck twice
First by light's finger, then by the malefactor known as ice.
As Elvis C. bleated in his nasal best, it's beyond belief, worse,
Because see here, there's Freudian anxiety at play, plus,
When we step inside, we see the Disneyfied idea of our selves
As interior lampoons; but the lamp's a false dawn,
As Diogenes, and his ilk, have instructed, on and on and on.
All I want is my mommy, but she's got cancer of the entirety,
Nor would a cure be possible, in this perplexity of bone,
Skin; I ache from aching at the ache of dying in my someone else.

July 11, 2024, London

Rule Britannia at the Proms...

Everything that made us great
Is gone
Except the right to repudiate
The sun
That never set upon Britannia
Once upon
A time when we were inhumane,
Spread out
Across bloodied time zones
Like a
Rare roast on a porcelain plate;
And that
Ability to finally decline to sing
The anthem
For the disappeared Atlantis of
Our past
Is the new realm we can inhabit
At least.
For some this will be more than
Enough,
But for most, it is the smallest cut
We can
Make in history's Imaginarium,
Spilling out
The seas of commerce, quarrel
As if
Smashing the lie of an aquarium.

we are wasted

something has misfired
the whole whizz and fret
of the awful gizmo is off —

like when children are
trapped on a stuck ride
for hours in moonlight.

That poem by Yeats

Good Friday is tomorrow,
when I was born —
tonight, on Amazon Prime
for one pound ninety-nine,
the retro passion
of *Jesus of Nazareth* glows
in the background.
The wind from that poem by Yeats
comes battering around like an actor
fired on the set for assault
and thrown instantly out
on their own devices.
I am too alone in my thoughts
to be at peace, Lord, blow down
my trees, I consider your storm,
and may well vote for it
when you call the election.

No great poem

No great poem

without something at stake:

the reach for the snake,

the Roman tree

about to break in three

Good Friday Sonnet

always the cross on the mind:
born there just as Jesus meant
us to be not, going forward —
their body an indivisible gatefold
kindness stretched to snap —
original, before ipseity —
image for what this bit does —
nothing stranger than
being the Word — opposite
of old language, to be truly true —
after Golgotha, no need
to prove love is catastrophe —
the chaos of the plan confuses
only any worldly, not wayward.

poetry is either a gift or a trick —

poetry is either a gift or a trick —
and let's not pretend
magic is our best friend.

sniper, you have no kindness

your minute freeze focus
is its own god, but one eye
is closed and another lies;
who will let you off
when you stop? who will pin
praise on cruel slow slyness?
worse, an easy finger is how
you make a new friend die —
hi little boy, playing girl —
you hollow shadow, sir
captain empty-soul, brrr
ghost-heart spider-breath,
you make sun sick to death,
your work trivial until you do it.

I listen to Ezra Koenig and read

a review of his new LP
in/on *The New Yorker* app

while stopped at Oxford uni
on a train filling up, *Urbis and Orbi*.

Pure Vampire Weekend pop.
I myself am a Gen-x flop.

Music Review of Superstar's LP

Other people exist, maybe.
T.S. Eliot recommended flight
from the personal. Advice not
taken, to put it mildly. Byron
perhaps is to blame — love
poetry has history. The hinge
of art is to avoid too much cringe
but risk some drowning;
we all scuttle in dreams, cough
sometimes in church; but war
is lurching forward across
our minds; is it possible to be
so self-known to not see
the heart is one story among
many; even if Troy flared up
due to passionate diapason,
arms and men concerned;
a few stars but it's not *Ulysses*,
but in a sense almost is.

Wanting shade even with sun,

Wanting shade even with sun,
we lie like appraisers on
a blanket weighted down
with cheese, bread, wine,
to look upwards at the green
appearances, how light is seen
through fingers of memory, one
leaf of cloud at a time; clean;
we love, say, long have we been
here this day; nothing, ah, done;
then it rains, we stay, not run —
no need to move yet, this is fine.

one can think of better things

one can think of better things
to do than take intravenous
penicillin for a tract infection,

sitting or lying on the slim bed
with wheels, apart from but
fixed on the half-blue sky

cut into architecture by windows
big as small cinema screens;
eventually, one is a Netflix

character in a classic remake —
a Weldon Kees Fifties man —
dapper, with a sense of style –

caught in an era's existential mix –
a whirlpool of desires —
film noir but brightly so, he is

lethargic, between the septic and the set-piece cure —
ovation as his chair rolls past clinical
fans, out to the waiting Imperial.

Boys In The Rain, 1982

All of us standing in the rain,
in our suits and ties, waiting

for a bus, or debating, skinny,
flawed, with impeccable hair

even in the rain, some with arms
big as The Thing, most stick thin,

a few derisory mustaches,
some cuter than girls, arrogant,

witty, flamboyant, anxious, yes,
a combustible enflavourment

to be sure, of all options, favours
deserved, or never served at all,

umbrellas rarely branched out,
hands free in wild proof-making.

Book of Idioms

Busy finding sand on the beach.
Having a hard time with lemons.
Not the timetables's best friend.
Splendid with new roller skates.
Completely at one with nettles.
The king's least favored PJs.
Selling used Bibles to atheists.
Juggling swordfish in a squall.
Dashing off with a short spoon.
Pitching tuna to a sick blowfish.
Advancing Himalayan theories.
Bringing a rock to a paper fight.

a syringe drifts by

a syringe drifts by
   light as a butterfly
     in a ballet attended
by all my former breakfasts —
   here comes a whirling
Marlowe in a tutu
with those nice socks
       patterned with clocks:

   shivering the seven seas
    onto my gown, in an electric
bed — halfway to the dead
we all belong to
   i remember what my mother
taught me — Frost's ends
of the world — me between ice
     fire piling its fists on —

the fever's hay-maker smiles —
   thank you thank you
for penicillin, this treatment —
   and the body and soul —
all hours coalesce in flushing
it out — if we make it out dear —
   let this suffice, suffice,
like riding out on our own device.

Gondoliers

when
i am gone
to lie down,
what will you do?
my poems all out
there,
long poles
playing canals,
the sounding
of sound —
dark green
green
the earth
all ears.

The Grand Minima

Totting it up a plethora of minuscule
debris fields, eon by inch,
the daily granular fractures,
chipped bits and bobs,
dust bunnies that don't ever quit,
the towering trivial pizza box
style of personal architecture —

love lies, business crops wilt, soar,
the whole a broken abacus possessed
by a stammering Ouija board
whose misspelt detritus inspires
poetry in the super-rich or bored,
the rising tide lifts all quotes, all toffs
step off yachts to sleep between sheets

when the port appears like a murdered
ghost — we host what we love most,
we live in a blackhole inside a blackhole,
like mice are denizens of a tinier Manhattan
project, the nuclearism is unclear, but here
it goes, small into smaller, like faller into fall or
inside the deep dive is the pool looping

around its Ouroboros dream of self —
we're colliding with the sun that grows us,
as dancers swoon in starlight to the violins
that thrill us with their spheres — oh musical
dividends, paying down, paying off,
jots and crosses, forgotten knots,
those broken rubber bands

good for nothing but snaking
about the lone chopstick, pennies
from Victor von Doom's homeland,
the whirligig pirouettes until it stops,
and we, who once were real, are legends
now for agents, booklet faces
left folded on the pews after the mourning,

some anecdotes might-as-well-be
Medieval, or, molecular iotas,
light liquified into cold solids, crazy
salad days browning definitively...
the rays that once were high as corn
now slowing down, so the small ice age
will waltz with rivers, on the planetary stage.

Lines from Verlaine

She plays with her cat
and to watch is to enjoy

how white hand and white paw
shadowbox as night deploys

all its dark laws and grim soldiery.
The kitten's a sly wide-boy,

hides like a villain in the game,
but carries fine sets of knives

in every hand, like Mack himself
armed to the teeth with skeng!

She can play nice, withdraw
her cat's triple-action claws,

razors any thinker would envy
but beware! — Satan lurks behind

the sweetest purr you may find,
while I listen in to my bae's laughs,

behind our green bedroom door,
wondering if beauty can ever beat

this beast's four iron-clad rapiers!

I was a cut-rate Cohen

who didn't play guitar.
I wanted to get to Heaven

but didn't get that far.
Now I'm in a Montmartre brothel

they claim's a five star hotel.
Lovers lie down in absinthe

but it doesn't make us fonder.
The rhyme scheme's shot to hell

and the spa's infernal lava.
I hear Oscar coughing next door

through wallpaper cheap and thin.
Wilde or Levant I can't tell.

The windmills are grinding redder,
the lamps are red as love: O

send Judas when you send thy dove.

My father when a young pop star

on the Decca label
around the time of 'Poetry
in Motion' appeared on TV
in a suit and tie to sing his hit
parade single 'Blue
and Lonely' — the show was
Like Young and he sang like
he meant it, while teenyboppers
danced on the set, the Sixties fun
transmitted to the homes
of Canadians across the land,
but especially into the one
in which my mother watched
her boyfriend Tom E. Swift, at
the swinging microphone; what
was not to like circa nineteen.

What hasn't happened yet

   We wait for
has already been
     time's doom-loop
spirals in terrible control —
   Paschal lamb, Pascal's wager —
it either is we will rise like Easter
     or lie forever unrenovated
forgotten mansions — from a rotten
   landlord.   spring ruins
winter — harrows hell — I renounce
my rational fears of being misled
by cant — because, I have lived
   in a world so crazy
nothing God could do or say
   sounds more improbable
than human history's lying men —
Pilate does not get my vote —
the women who witnessed
     that empty tomb today back then –
were not credible witnesses —
which accentuates the smack of reality –
something out there did
occur — weird, enough to drive Rome
to worship the lowest weirdo ever —
   love comes and goes / stays
in a whirlpool at the sun's odd core.

among the paintings

cool modernism
i can lie down without people
in the frame,
and feel the itself of things,
their beauty without noise /
it is comforting
to be alone with art,
after all the lies of men —
so futile, so energized! —
not even whispering,
not even experimental punctuation
that makes the rain oblique /
nothing is more quiet
than a factory by Ault —
the blue-lit windows at night
unbroken by human figures
in the umber evening of Hoboken.

We stopped writing about Easter

When our tree ran out of gas;
The eggs warmed; the crosses burned.
Buns sued Maine. The bunny made ominous
Threats towards Greenland. The parade

Turned itself into a hatchet, and dug itself out
Of the grave. The land gave up its dead,
And not in a good way. Friday went backwards,
And the living died like they were in dubious prison

For the criminally bald. The mild weather
Spoke ill of old Europe, and the wind sang
About the merry days of ruination in the markets.
The cherry blossoms stopped at every border,

To pay for themselves with their own vanishing;
Fear went freelance like a befurred farrier,
The dangling promises hung themselves out to dry,
And no one woke to find anything sweet hidden

In plain sight, it was all very unclear where any
Of us were; and then Romans handed us nails,
Some non-Canadian wood, ordered us
To vote with our blows, which brought in a landslide

Of blood and flesh, pouring out of the human basket,
As if one of our fellow men was a grocery list,
Being pulled out of its own skin, to make pain
The national dessert, in the moment of golden praise.

Maundy Thursday, Easter, 2025

The currency I traded in

Is bearish now, at fifty-nine
My volatility index has squandered
Its lows and highs, is in decline —
The lyric force is muted by the times,
Which lie like bricklayers build brick
To brick — as that song went, another
And another — that was the image,
If I recall, from dark gyms, at fourteen
Or so, terrified to dance slow, or quick,
With those around me on the walls;
Music, that brings us back to ourselves,
Takes us out to sea as well,
Like a drug that can murder or revive;
What language can I use to defend a form,
A rhetoric, even, that has been designed
To crush whole peoples, sign by sign?
Tanks roll on, drones scour the air like hawks,
To hurt the ones below, but only poetry kills
By sound or fine-bonded lines. To me,
What's serene or boundless in a poem thrills,
But it advances in English, crushes like a love
That will not slow dance to urgency in grade nine.
The world was bad in sixty-six, has always been,
One supposes, ruled by the maniac fixed on deformities
Of the soul, that no plastic arts can reshape to good;
But at this peak of my presence, albeit stumbling,
I can locate, as if to blow apart, on the unsafe ground,
A collective malice in the blood, like perfume,
Except an odour of varied virulent sprays, wafting
Over borders like a gas; what can we do, who mask
Ourselves with words, to play for better futures?
I have listened to the sleepless inkwell night,

And dipping into the inexplicable infinites of minus
Light, have understood a signal from the solar winds:
It says, in no language but of mathematics, or the divine,
As if Bach had been a hole that whorled back into sight,
Bring on the great floods, make the world without form again,
So in the weird stillness before creation a differing biology
Can think itself into manifestation on an open canvas,
Rebirth of all that struggles, fights knives out, without cease.

April 8, 2025

On Goya

Black days, black days
the good dog drowns
in a river gone mud brown,
a father tears his own son's
blood out of his head —
the peasants of the town,
on feast day no less, loll
their stupid mouths and eyes,
full-idiotic, semi-cartoon —
endless puss-stream of devil
following buffoons, ominous
when not comical, oblivious
to any palette of the sun dial,
a burnt-blunted smudge face
as if soot was given life-evil,
like dumb malice was incarnated
here in Madrid, to be displayed
only in private, while close above,
bright smart as a magpie's hoard,
riding purebred stallions rearing,
hatted hunting with loyal hounds,
the royal good and great appear,
unknowing their author also
creates a true picture of offal, strife,
excrement, war, heart-beating clubs
as brother kills brother forever,
beneath the shimmers of silver,
deep vein reds, vermillion breasts
on which gold pinned medals glow —
limning the divine, grosser
superfluities, oozing grimaces given
formal presence, white bone below

bright skin of favor, gentility, is smeared art —
crushed vicious paint,
true emergent deformities seen,
if unrevealed, yet like bad God was
deaf, blind, blunt force cruel,
as if beauty paid the bills upstairs,
while bestial capering incivility
was the real order of the dark day.

The only love that never lies

The only love that never lies
is when a book takes by surprise
your every hour, each stolen look,
and evenings fly,
as if a sweetened hook
came from above
to complicate your eyes'
true mind — it overtakes,
it floods, it knows you as you:
heart, soul, body shook —
it says I am your best of lovers —
nothing else tastes even half as good,
not even jam as what's so deep
within those new tempting covers.

haven't been here in a while

haven't been here in a while
here being this subset of things
wherein a line of symbols sings
like a vibrating string strung
between two tin cans, set
thrumming by a bird landing
in the middle of the wiring,
twinned ears listening in like
spies on a hidden wireless
inside a bible in a Somerset
barn during the war, when
it mattered what side you batted
for — sides matter again now again it's true —
those twins I drew leaning out
of conjoined windows to hear words of
contact like on the moon —
crackling noise barely saying love,
but getting it across the line
like a marathon runner
dying just after making it to the ribbon
first, breaking to win,
the race to say I know you do first;
And so here I am, your sound burst

I shoot the rose

Nothing very tricky, no need
here for filter or other glossy
plays — this self-complex
involvement of every good
turns on lips never smirking
with glamour's irony: roses
are sincere, even if they hurt
in places — skin-prick — eye —
only stand and frame, even
a bit offhand — then take —

this displaced star is colour,
scent, stillness and petals falling

like water in winter — a gown.
Nothing before prepares one
for a rose; and after, having been bitten
by their frenzy of terrible calm,
their inner lives
knowing that nothing else is more
than what they offer —
we live always alert, on the lookout for
their next, appalling appearance
uncontrollable and serene.

The Mole Man

Who else smears themselves
With honey for the fire ants,
Lies down to await their doom?
It's loathing of ourselves
That capsizes yachts, that Hindenburgs
Our airships. We immolate
So often, furious our armaments
Are depleting, short supply a shellshock
Of sorts in this war for attention,
A sense of deep ocean failure, deeper
Than where trying bathyspheres implode,
Some kind of limit named for a great mind,
So deep the finest mines explode as they descend;
I enter my own suffering with something like
A goal-oriented sprint each day — a Mole Man
Burrowing down to the solid core,
Past the impenetrable lava, which my intricate
Goggles intercept and defray on pain of dying.

Arizona

There is a place in Arizona
I have never been
I can picture —

Out of the motel, sun:
I am happy here
And more — serene —

Without any backstory,
Just entering the day
Like a scene

Pleased to be imagining
Clarity of a life
Lived elsewhere, stolen

From encumbrances,
Stripped down for parts —
A chassis by the roadside

A life picked clean, doing fine.

Sonnet for obscure makers

There are no shrines to failed poets,
On the shores of wintry provinces —
No prizes for lost conductors, gone
Inward on pine needles deep in tundra —
The arts combine like military forces
To defeat the weak unknown, valorise
A winning side; but B-side people live too,
Drunk on cedar wine, porcupine stew,
Entangled leaves after autumn first —
We tried and did not make our mark —
Fell too soon or up and died — forgotten,
Our songs and words for god or lover
Wounded too few or none at all — so we
Are not saints, though we also bled for passion.

I have not done justice to my mother

I have not done justice to my mother,
The sweep of her life,
How when young, she was young,
In a country, on a farm, and other children,

And I will never know their names,
I have forgotten to ask so much,
How lazy have I been! Now that she is going,
Out of this room, where we can see her,

Where she can be talked with, now that she is
Leaving the scene of all our disputations,
All the tomfoolery of this world, and the music
She listened to, her cooking, her reading,

Her studies at McGill, those meticulously marked
Textbooks, the kisses, the childbirth, the sons,
Jordan, the colds, the flying to China,
The mourning, lovemaking, waking to make instant

Coffee, the long discussions about serial killers,
About our ancestors, about Uncle Sandy and Port
Daniel, the summers, the winters, the cross-country
Skiing, the wedding photos, the modelling career,

The rages, the laughing, sometimes, the criticism
Of certain TV shows, the gardening, love of dogs,
The love of cats, the swimming out so far,
I have not done justice to my mother,

I must begin to make a start of it, this gathering
Of what her life was, and somehow, compress it all
Into a space no bigger than a page, or some earth,
Or a leaf, like the one she sent me, from Canada,

Upon hearing I could not have children; and why do we
Try to capture a life, tell a story of a life, what is our concern?
Are we sad at the going, at the losing, at the constriction
Of our knowledge, our chances to learn more?

I know nothing I was not told, or didn't see,
I am trying to do justice, as if an injustice has been done,
And I think it has been – I think such a person, so much
Of her being taken away, all at once – I find it monstrous,

And I know it is the way of all things, the rushing away,
The ruination of our snow forts with the first sunbursts of April,
I see it all, the quarrels, the lost opportunities, the love
Of Cohen, Trudeau (*père*), of trees, and lakes, of rain,

The love of the sea, the love of travel, of her husband,
The few friends, the strong views, the constant searching
For lineage, for ancestry, for a sense of belonging, her life,
Her father the great tall pole-vaulter, her stern smart mother,

Her brother, her sisters, her childhood among animals,
Born during the second world war, born at the worst moment,
Somehow surviving, falling in love, young mother in a sportscar,
How did you do it, how did it all come together, and all the papers,

The collected, curated papers, and documents, the careful study,
The years of mourning, the years of swimming, this
I can only summarise, list like Whitman, who you loved,
Especially his lilacs, when they last bloomed, and do so here again,

As I ask them to appear, as I ask all of Lincoln's lilacs to come
To surround your dying time, to bear you up, and flow around you,
In their mystery, in their scent, as you are deserving of no less,
As you are my mother, and I thank you, finally, with the flowers

THE GRAND MINIMA

From the poem you read me, how often, thank you, how poetry
Flowed from you to me, the electric gift you gave, and saved me with.

December 8, 2024, London

Bio

Todd Swift has a PhD and was born in Montreal on Good Friday, 1966.
At school and university, he was a champion debater.
In his 20s he wrote TV screenplays for Disney, Paramount, HBO, etc.
He was also a longtime emcee for various cabarets in Montreal,
    Budapest and Paris.
He was Oxfam poet in residence for a decade.
He is married, and has lived in London, UK, for over 20 years.
He is the author of over a dozen collections of poetry.
He has edited and co-edited many anthologies.
He was Poet-in-residence at Pembroke College, Cambridge 2017-2018,
    and third placed runner up for the Oxford Professor of Poetry.
He has been a publisher since 2012.
He has a blood clot on his heart, and a CRT-D device implanted.
He loves cats, walking, swimming, coffee, and talking in cafes.
He also loves movies, music, and food.
And his friends, and books. And penguins, and socks, and
    Swatch watches.
Probably: cats, books, swimming, coffee, and a blizzard is a top 5.
Sitting by a fireplace with a book and cat and coffee with a blizzard
    outside, basically.

Acknowledgements

None of these poems were commissioned, or published anywhere else by anyone else, except on the author's own socials, and all were composed on an iPhone in 2024 and 2025.

Thank you to wonderful Sara; and my doctors and nurses, and to my friend, the artist and poet, and book designer, Edwin Smet. And, the key cat, beloved Suetonius, who turned nine years old in April 2025.

A selected list of the author's previous poetry collections and pamphlets of the past 25 years

Budavox Poems 1990-1999 (DC Books, Canada, 1999)

Seaway New & Selected Poems (Salmon Poetry, Ireland, 2008)

The Ministry of Emergency Situations: Selected Poems
(Marick Press, USA, 2014)

Madness & Love in Maida Vale (Eyewear, UK, 2016)

Dream-beauty-psycho (Eyewear, UK, 2017)

There's An Excess at the Heart of Being That's Wild (Eyewear, UK, 2019)

Spring In Name Only (Eyewear, UK, 2020)

Opening Hours (Maida Vale, UK, 2021)

Last Poems Before Heart Failure (Maida Vale, UK, 2022)

Optician to the Stars: New Poems 2022-2023 (Maida Vale, UK, 2024)

Past praise for earlier collections

'[...] a dapper sense of style' – Emily Berry

'[...] uncommon panache and intelligence' – Srikanth Reddy

'A voice for our time' – Derek Mahon

'His voice is powerfully his own, but poetry lovers will find the grace notes of plainsong TS Eliot, but also the verbal dexterity of Robert Bringhurst' – George Elliott Clarke

'Sincerity and comedy attuned to a subtle ear' – Daljit Nagra

'Some of his lyric moments are joyously Audenesque'
– Fiona Sampson

'Swift has a beautiful sense of the rhythm of the English language' – Pericles Lewis

'Swift is a prodigiously talented and singular poet' – Don Share

'Swift's work is as playful as serious work gets to be'
– David Lehman

'Todd Swift is a poet besotted with language and stubbornly working out a high style of his own' – Al Alvarez

'Todd Swift is a revelation' – Terrance Hayes

'Todd Swift is the real thing' – Ilya Kaminsky

www.ingramcontent.com/pod-product-compliance
Ingram Content Group UK Ltd.
Pitfield, Milton Keynes, MK11 3LW, UK
UKHW041843170625
459785UK00002B/2